# little Miss Somersault

by Roger Hargreaves

Little Miss Somersault is the sort of person who doesn't just go out for a walk.

Oh no, not Little Miss Somersault.

She is too full of energy for that.

Rather than walking everywhere, she cartwheels everywhere!

She doesn't just walk through her front door.

That would be too easy.

She built a house where she could climb
over the roof first!

Little Miss Somersault doesn't just sit in a chair.

She balances on the back of it.

Little Miss Somersault doesn't walk around things.

She jumps right over them!

And rather than answer the telephone
like you or I might, she...

...well, just look at her!

The other day, when she was cartwheeling past
Mr Worry's house, he called out to her.
"There's a leaf on my roof. Please could
you get it for me?" he asked.

Mr Worry had spent the whole morning worrying
that the leaf might make his roof fall in!

"I have a long ladder," he added.

Little Miss Somersault said, "I don't need a ladder."
And, quick as a flash, she climbed on top of
Mr Worry's house and got the leaf off.

A little further down the lane,
Little Miss Somersault came to
Mr Skinny's house.

Mr Skinny was at the top of a ladder,
painting his roof.

Unfortunately, Mr Bump came around the corner and walked under the ladder.

Or rather, he tried to walk under the ladder, but being Mr Bump he walked straight into it.

BUMP!

And you can see what happened!

Little Miss Somersault had seen it all happen.

And without a thought for the ladder lying on
the ground, she climbed to the top of
Mr Skinny's house and carried him
safely to the ground,
under her arm.

He wasn't very heavy!

By the next morning, everybody had heard
about Little Miss Somersault's daring deeds.

The phone rang. It was Mr Uppity.
"There's an umbrella stuck in my chimney.
I hear you're good at climbing onto roofs.
I'll expect you here in five minutes!"

Mr Uppity's house is one of the biggest
houses you will ever have seen.

"To climb to the top of Mr Uppity's house
would be a real challenge," said
Little Miss Somersault.

It took no time at all for Little Miss Somersault
to climb on to Mr Uppity's roof.

"That was easy," she said, as she
balanced on a chimney pot.

Then she looked down at the ground, far below her.

That was the last thing she should have done.
Little Miss Somersault suddenly felt dizzy.
Her knees began to tremble.
Everything began to spin round and round.

Little Miss Somersault had discovered she
was afraid of heights!

Luckily, Mr Tickle happened to be passing.

He stretched out one of his
extraordinarily long arms.

Do you think he wanted to tickle
Little Miss Somersault?

Of course he did!

But not before he had brought her back
safely down to the ground.

"Stop it!" laughed Little Miss Somersault.
"I promise I won't do anything so foolish again!"

And off went Mr Tickle to look for
somebody else to tickle.

That evening, Little Miss Somersault was sitting, that's right, sitting, in her armchair.

Suddenly the telephone rang.

"My hat has blown off," said a voice at the other end. "And it's landed on the roof of my house. Could you..."

Little Miss Somersault's face turned pale.

"Who is this?" she asked, in a trembling voice.

"It's Mr Small," said Mr Small.

Little Miss Somersault breathed a
huge sigh of relief.

"I'll be there in five minutes!" she said.

And off she somersaulted!

# 3 Great Offers for MR.MEN Fans!

MR.MEN TOKEN

## 1 New Mr. Men or Little Miss Library Bus Presentation Cases

A brand new stronger, roomier school bus library box, with sturdy carrying handle and stay-closed fasteners.

The full colour, wipe-clean boxes make a great home for your full collection.

They're just £5.99 inc P&P and free bookmark!

☐ MR. MEN  ☐ LITTLE MISS (please tick and order overleaf)

MR.MEN
Library Bus!

PLEASE
STICK YOUR
50P COIN
HERE

## 2 Door Hangers and Posters

In every Mr. Men and Little Miss book like this one, you will find a special token. Collect 6 tokens and we will send you a brilliant Mr. Men or Little Miss poster and a Mr. Men or Little Miss double sided full colour bedroom door hanger of your choice. Simply tick your choice in the list and tape a 50p coin for your two items to this page.

**Door Hangers** (please tick)
☐ Mr. Nosey & Mr. Muddle
☐ Mr. Slow & Mr. Busy
☐ Mr. Messy & Mr. Quiet
☐ Mr. Perfect & Mr. Forgetful
☐ Little Miss Fun & Little Miss Late
☐ Little Miss Helpful & Little Miss Tidy
☐ Little Miss Busy & Little Miss Brainy
☐ Little Miss Star & Little Miss Fun

**Posters** (please tick)
☐ MR.MEN
☐ LITTLE MISS

# 3 Sixteen Beautiful Fridge Magnets – any 2 for £2.00!
inc.P&P

They're very special collector's items!
Simply tick your first and second* choices from the list below
of any 2 characters!

## 1st Choice

- [ ] Mr. Happy
- [ ] Mr. Lazy
- [ ] Mr. Topsy-Turvy
- [ ] Mr. Bounce
- [ ] Mr. Bump
- [ ] Mr. Small
- [ ] Mr. Snow
- [ ] Mr. Wrong

- [ ] Mr. Daydream
- [ ] Mr. Tickle
- [ ] Mr. Greedy
- [ ] Mr. Funny
- [ ] Little Miss Giggles
- [ ] Little Miss Splendid
- [ ] Little Miss Naughty
- [ ] Little Miss Sunshine

## 2nd Choice

- [ ] Mr. Happy
- [ ] Mr. Lazy
- [ ] Mr. Topsy-Turvy
- [ ] Mr. Bounce
- [ ] Mr. Bump
- [ ] Mr. Small
- [ ] Mr. Snow
- [ ] Mr. Wrong

- [ ] Mr. Daydream
- [ ] Mr. Tickle
- [ ] Mr. Greedy
- [ ] Mr. Funny
- [ ] Little Miss Giggles
- [ ] Little Miss Splendid
- [ ] Little Miss Naughty
- [ ] Little Miss Sunshine

*Only in case your first choice is out of stock.

CUT ALONG DOTTED LINE AND RETURN THIS WHOLE PAGE

---

**TO BE COMPLETED BY AN ADULT**

**To apply for any of these great offers, ask an adult to complete the coupon below and send it with the appropriate payment and tokens, if needed, to MR. MEN OFFERS, PO BOX 7, MANCHESTER M19 2HD**

- [ ] Please send _____ Mr. Men Library case(s) and/or_____ Little Miss Library case(s) at £5.99 each inc P&P
- [ ] Please send a poster and door hanger as selected overleaf. I enclose six tokens plus a 50p coin for P&P
- [ ] Please send me _____ pair(s) of Mr. Men/Little Miss fridge magnets, as selected above at £2.00 inc P&P

**Fan's Name** _____

**Address** _____

_____ **Postcode** _____

**Date of Birth** _____

**Name of Parent/Guardian** _____

**Total amount enclosed £**_____

- [ ] **I enclose a cheque/postal order payable to Egmont Books Limited**
- [ ] **Please charge my MasterCard/Visa/Amex/Switch or Delta account** (delete as appropriate)

| | | | | | | | | | | | | | | | | |
|--|--|--|--|--|--|--|--|--|--|--|--|--|--|--|--|--|

Card Number

**Expiry date** ___/___   **Signature** _____

Please allow 28 days for delivery. We reserve the right to change the terms of this offer at any time but we offer a 14 day money back guarantee. This does not affect your statutory rights.